THE CAUSES OF WORLD WAR II

ALEXANDER OFFORD

 Crabtree Publishing Company

www.crabtreebooks.com

Author: Alexander Offord

Publishing plan research and development: Crabtree Publishing Company

Editors: Jackie Dell, Lynn Peppas

Proofreaders: Kelly Stern, Wendy Scavuzzo

Editorial services: Clarity Content Services

Production coordinator and prepress technician: Tammy McGarr

Print coordinator: Margaret Amy Salter

Series consultant: Fayaz Chagani

Cover design: Ken Wright

Design: David Montle

Photo Research: Linda Tanaka

Front cover: Portrait of German leader Adolf Hitler
Title page: Members of the German Waffen-SS march in formation during the Nuremberg Rally in September 1937
Contents page: Russian leader Vladimir Ilyich Ulyanov, more commonly known as Lenin; USS Arizona burning after the Japanese attack on Pearl Harbor; Italian leader Benito Amilcare Andrea Mussolini

Photo Credits:
Front cover: Bridgeman Images: Private Collection / Archives Charmet;
Back cover: Wikimedia: public domain
Title page Everett Historical/Shutterstock; p3 top PD/Russia, The US National Archives and Records Administration/195617, PD/wikipedia; p4 Everett Historical/Shutterstock; p5 PD/US Gov/American Battle Monuments Commission; p6 Public Domain; p9 USDOE/National Nuclear Security Administration; p10 Library of Congress/USZC4-10890; p11 IWM/Q 20633; p12 top Library of Congress/LC-USZC4-12412, PD/Clemenceau by Celia Beaux,1920, David Lloyd George by George William Orpen/wikipedia; p13 Library of Congress/LC-USZ62-113662; p14 *The Democratic banner*. (Mt. Vernon, Ohio), 24 June 1919. *Chronicling America: Historic American Newspapers*/Library of Congress/sn88078751; p15 PD/*The Signing of Peace in the Hall of Mirrors, Versailles, 28ᵗʰ June 1919* by George William Orpen/Google Art Project; p16 *New-York Tribune*. (New York [N.Y.]), 23 June 1919. *Chronicling America: Historic American Newspapers*/Library of Congress/Sn83030214; p18 US Gov; p19 © Punch Limited; p20 PD/Russia; p21 PD/Ephraim Stillberg/Museum Batumi/CC-BY-3.0; p22 wikipedia; p23 top PD/Japan, inset PD/Japan; pp24-25 PD/Italy; p25 PD/wikipedia; p26 PD/ww2database; p27 PD/Bundesarchiv, Bild 119-11-19-12; p28 Library of Congress/LC-USZ62-123429; p29 PD/US Gov; p30 top National Archives Canada/4240259, National Archives Canada/4240334, US National Oceanic and Atmospheric Administration; p31 PD/Wikimedia; p34 Released to Public Domain by owner; p35 London Illustrated/London News and Sketch; p37 Pictures from History/Bridgeman Images; p38 US Gov/US Navy; p39 US National Archives/USA C-5904; p40 Bundesarchiv, DVM 10 Bild 23-63-40/CC-BY-SA; p42 US National Archives.

t=Top, bl=Bottom Left, br=Bottom Right

Library and Archives Canada Cataloguing in Publication

Offord, Alexander, author
    The causes of World War II / Alexander Offord.

(World War II : history's deadliest conflict)
Includes index.
Issued in print and electronic formats.
ISBN 978-0-7787-2116-1 (bound).--ISBN 978-0-7787-2120-8 (paperback).--ISBN 978-1-4271-1698-7 (pdf).--ISBN 978-1-4271-1694-9 (html)

    1. World War, 1939-1945--Causes--Juvenile literature. I. Title.

D741.O44 2015   j940.53'11   C2015-904382-4
                                                          C2015-904383-2

Library of Congress Cataloging-in-Publication Data

Offord, Alexander.
    The causes of World War II / Alexander Offord.
       pages cm. -- (World War II: history's deadliest conflict)
    Includes index.
    ISBN 978-0-7787-2116-1 (reinforced library binding) --
      ISBN 978-0-7787-2120-8 (pbk.) --
      ISBN 978-1-4271-1698-7 (electronic pdf) --
      ISBN 978-1-4271-1694-9 (electronic html)
    1. World War, 1939-1945--Causes--Juvenile literature. I. Title.

D741.O35 2015
940.53'11--dc23
                                                     2015023295

Crabtree Publishing Company

www.crabtreebooks.com   1-800-387-7650   Printed in Canada/112015/EF20150911

Copyright © **2016 CRABTREE PUBLISHING COMPANY**. All rights reserved. No part of this publication may be reproduced, stored in a retrieval system or be transmitted in any form or by any means, electronic, mechanical, photocopying, recording, or otherwise, without the prior written permission of Crabtree Publishing Company. In Canada: We acknowledge the financial support of the Government of Canada through the Canada Book Fund for our publishing activities.

Published in Canada
Crabtree Publishing
616 Welland Ave.
St. Catharines, Ontario
L2M 5V6

Published in the United States
Crabtree Publishing
PMB 59051
350 Fifth Avenue, 59th Floor
New York, New York 10118

Published in the United Kingdom
Crabtree Publishing
Maritime House
Basin Road North, Hove
BN41 1WR

Published in Australia
Crabtree Publishing
3 Charles Street
Coburg North
VIC, 3058

CONTENTS

INTRODUCTION
The Last War? — 4

CHAPTER 1
Post-WWI Treaties — 10

CHAPTER 2
Political Shifts Post-WWI — 20

CHAPTER 3
The Great Depression and Global Economic Decline — 28

CHAPTER 4
Invasions and Occupations — 32

CHAPTER 5
Pacts and Alliances — 40

CONCLUSION
The Long Road to War — 42

FURTHER READING AND WEBSITES — 45

GLOSSARY — 46

INDEX — 48

INTRODUCTION

THE LAST WAR?

In 1918, World War I—then called the Great War—came to an end. The victors were an alliance of countries known as the **Allied powers**, also called the Triple Entente. It included British Empire, French Republic, and the Russian Empire, along with other allies such as Italy, Japan, and the United States.

The **Axis powers**, also known as the Central Powers, had been defeated. They were an alliance of countries that included Germany, Austria-Hungary, Bulgaria, and the **Ottoman Empire**.

BELOW: *Germany stopped fighting on November 11, 1918, and accepted defeat.*

ABOVE: The American Memorial at the cemetery at Flanders Field in Belgium honors the soldiers who died fighting in World War I.

THE LEGACY OF WWI

After four years of bombings, much of Europe had been destroyed. Many of the buildings in famous cities such as London and Paris lay in pieces. Many roads and bridges had been damaged, and farmland across the continent had been torn up.

In some countries, such as Britain, food was so scarce that the government began a policy of rationing. This made sure all citizens received only a small amount of food each day to keep the nation from running out of food.

In Austria-Hungary alone, nearly two million people had been left homeless because of the war. Worst of all, an estimated 37 million people worldwide had been killed.

PEACE AT LAST?

Because so many countries had been involved in WWI, many people believed that the end of the war would bring about world peace. In fact, the war was not called "World War I" or "the First World War" until World War II began, because in 1918, people assumed they would never see another conflict the size of the Great War. Unfortunately, that war and the events that came afterward actually set the stage for an even bigger world war.

ABOVE: *On top of everything else, the Great Depression of the 1930s brought more economic hardships to people who were still recovering from the war. People often stood in line for free food.*

THE WORLD AFTER WWI

WWI had many causes, but it officially started after the assassination of Austrian archduke Franz Ferdinand. Because the assassination took place on Serbian soil, Austria blamed Serbia. After the war, the Allied forces continued to blame the Axis powers for causing the war. The Allies agreed that the defeated countries should return any land they had taken over, and pay for the damage the war had caused. On their side, the Axis powers felt the punishments they received were too harsh. They resented the Allies in return. This anger among nations only got stronger over the 20 years that followed WWI.

> " This, the greatest of all wars, is not just another war — it is the last war! "
>
> —BRITISH WRITER H.G. WELLS, WRITING ABOUT WORLD WAR I

Changing Borders

One reason that conflict kept growing in Europe was the desire for more land and more power. Some countries thought that by controlling other countries, they could prevent another war. Other countries believed they had a right to claim land that had been taken away from them. One country could control another through three different means.

One way was **annexation**, where one country conquers territory in another country, and claims that territory as part of itself. For example, in 1938, Germany annexed Austria.

A country could also control another country through a **mandate** from the **League of Nations**, which was like today's **United Nations**. For example, in 1939 Britain had a mandate over the middle-eastern territory of Palestine, which meant that Britain governed the people of Palestine.

Finally, one country could control another country by creating a **colony**. A colony is a country that is politically and economically controlled by another country. For example, Canada and the United States both began as colonies of Britain and France.

LEFT: *Before 1939, many of the countries we recognize today didn't exist. They were controlled by, or were part of, other countries. This map shows the borders in Europe before World War II.*

What do you think?
Should countries be allowed to take control of other countries? If so, why?

WORLD WAR II BEGINS

During the 1920s and 1930s, some countries changed the way they governed their citizens. Countries that had similar governments formed new alliances and broke old ones. By 1939, the composition of the Allied powers and the Axis powers had gone through many changes. In that year, the Allied powers consisted of Australia, Britain, Canada, France, India, New Zealand, Poland, and South Africa. On the other side, Germany, Italy, and Japan formed the Axis powers.

World War II began on September 2, 1939, after Germany invaded the tiny country of Poland. Poland was an ally of Britain and France, which both declared war on Germany.

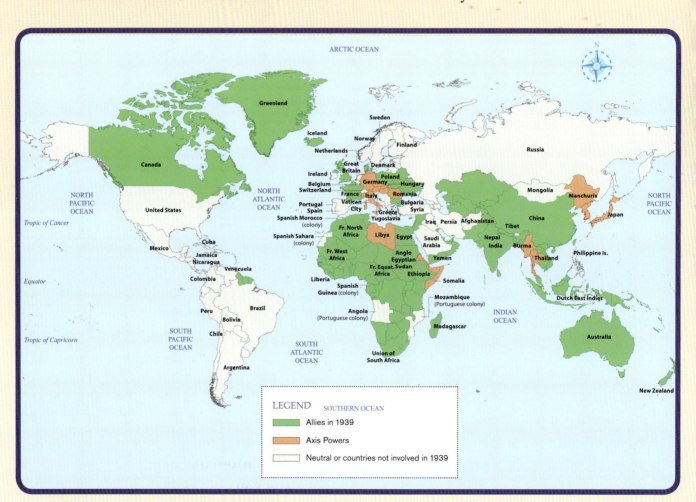

ABOVE: *Allied, Axis, and neutral countries in 1939*

ABOVE: *The invention of the atomic bomb has affected international relations up to the present day.*

The Scale of Destruction

For the next six years, a conflict raged whose destruction surpassed that of the Great War. Empires rose and fell, friendly nations became enemies, and some enemies became friends. Battles were fought on land, at sea, and in the air. The war was fought in three major areas, called **fronts**. The fronts were Europe, the Pacific, and the Middle East, which included parts of North Africa.

New technologies led to better boats, submarines, weapons, tanks, and airplanes on both sides. World War II also brought the invention of the most terrible weapon ever created: the **atomic bomb**. According to some estimates, more than 15 million soldiers were killed during WWII, with an additional 25 million wounded. More than 45 million **civilians** were also killed during WWII, including the six million victims of the tragic Jewish **Holocaust**.

CHAPTER 1
POST-WWI TREATIES

World War I ended at 11 a.m. on November 11, 1918, when Germany signed the **Armistice of Compiègne**. An armistice is a formal agreement between two countries to stop fighting. The Armistice of Compiègne was the first of many **treaties**, agreements, and documents made to ensure a lasting world peace. Some nations resented the treaties, however, and either thought they were too harsh or not harsh enough. Instead of peace, the treaties helped to cause another world war.

ATTITUDES AFTER WWI

Many people in the Allied countries believed that Germany should be punished for its involvement in World War I. Politicians in the Allied countries were aware of that. In 1918, David Lloyd George was re-elected as Britain's prime minister on the promise that he would "make Germany pay."

Blaming Germany

Before World War I, Britain was the most powerful nation in the world. It had colonies all over the globe and a large navy. After the war, the navy was severely damaged, and many of Britain's colonies had been attacked by Germany and its allies. This was a huge shock to the British people, who were used to being the strongest nation in the world. It created a great deal of anger in British citizens.

French citizens also felt the same anger. Their country had been invaded by Germany, and the French people now felt vulnerable and were afraid of a future attack.

RIGHT: *Posters like this one were common during and after WWI.*

LEFT: *The Allied naval blockade extended a year beyond the end of WWI to ensure Germany was crippled.*

Resenting the Allies

On their side, many Germans were feeling humiliated because they had lost the war. Besides that, much of the land that made up the German Empire had been taken away from them. Germany was also expected to pay the Allies billions of dollars to make up for the damages of the war. As a result, Germans felt great anger and resentment toward the Allied nations.

A CRIPPLED EUROPE

In all, it is estimated that the Allies spent more than $125 billion (in American dollars) on the war, and that the Axis powers spent $60 billion. Both sides had suffered many casualties and were nearly broke. In some European countries, the destruction of farmland and trade routes led to widespread food shortages. Some countries, such as Britain, had to create special food-rationing laws to keep from running out. Germany, in particular, had been suffering from an Allied naval blockade, which prevented ships carrying food and other supplies from reaching the German people. The blockade lasted from 1915 to 1919. In all, an estimated 424,000 Germans died from starvation and disease because of the blockade.

What Do You Know?

Many Americans believed they shouldn't have gone to war in the first place. WWI was considered a "European war" that the United States had no business taking part in. When the war was over, most Americans were tired of getting involved overseas. They believed that they should only concern themselves with problems on American soil. This belief is called **isolationism**.

THE PARIS PEACE CONFERENCE

When World War I ended in 1918, representatives from many countries gathered in Paris, France. This gathering of nations was called the **Paris Peace Conference** and was held in the famous Palace of Versailles. The goal of the conference was to settle old disagreements between nations to create a lasting peace. Not every nation was invited, however. The Russian government and none of the defeated Axis nations were allowed to participate. Even so, the Paris Peace Conference was full of fierce debate, since every country that attended believed it was being treated unfairly.

The Big Three

The three most influential representatives were from France, Britain, and the United States. These were now the three wealthiest and most powerful nations, and they each wanted something different. The French prime minister, Georges Clemenceau, wanted to make sure Germany never rose to power again. Sharing a border with Germany made France especially vulnerable to attack. He also wanted Germany to return the provinces of Alsace and Lorraine, which it had taken from France. Clemenceau earned the nickname "the Tiger" because of his strong beliefs. He thought Germany should be punished for its role in WWI.

This brought him into conflict with the American president, Woodrow Wilson, who had another plan. During the war, Wilson created his famous Fourteen Points, which outlined a vision of peace for the post-war world.

The British prime minister, David Lloyd George, was somewhere in the middle. He wanted to punish Germany, but he knew that if the punishment was too harsh, peace would not last.

RIGHT: *American president Woodrow Wilson won the Nobel Peace Prize in 1919 for his work at the Paris Peace Conference.*

LEFT: *This photograph shows Georges Clemenceau, prime minister of France, during the Paris Peace Conference.*

RIGHT: *David Lloyd George served as prime minister of Britain from 1916 to 1922, leading Britain through the end of WWI.*

The Fourteen Points

Woodrow Wilson's Fourteen Points had a large influence on the outcome of the conference. They were created in 1918 when Wilson asked one of his advisers to gather 150 experts to figure out the best way to ensure peace after the war. This group of experts was called the **Inquiry**. After several months of work by the Inquiry, President Wilson presented the Fourteen Points to Congress.

The most important points were the first five and the last one. The first five points applied to all the nations of the world. The rest had to do with individual countries. Point one called for open diplomacy, which meant that countries would no longer make agreements in secret. Point two called for freedom of the seas, so that no country could own the ocean.

Point three demanded the removal of economic barriers, so that no country would have to pay more for goods than any other country. Point four asked all nations to get rid of their weapons to prevent a future war. Point five asked that all the colonies of the world be investigated to determine to whom they really belonged.

Finally, point 14 called for the creation of an international League of Nations. This was Woodrow Wilson's favorite of the 14 points. He fought hard to create the League at the Paris Peace Conference, even allowing for some exceptions to the first five points. For example, Britain would only join the League if there was no freedom of the seas. Woodrow Wilson accepted.

BELOW: *This photograph shows Woodrow Wilson delivering the Fourteen Points to Congress.*

THE TREATY OF VERSAILLES

The Paris Peace Conference ended on June 28, 1919, after almost a full year of negotiations. Finally, the most important treaty of WWI was signed: the **Treaty of Versailles**. The document was long and detailed, and officially ended the war between Germany and the Allies. The agreements made in the Treaty of Versailles caused big changes in the lives of ordinary Germans and created the tension and resentment that led to WWII.

The Treaty of Versailles required that Germany give up most of the new territory it had claimed during the war. In all, that added up to more than 25,000 square miles (64,750 square km) of land and a population of seven million people. In the process, German colonies in China and what is now Rwanda were divided between Britain and France. Belgium and Czechoslovakia regained their independence.

The treaty also required Germany to give some of its coal mines to France. Germany had destroyed so many French coal mines during the war that France could no longer produce enough of the resource. It was agreed that France would have complete access to certain German coal mines for a period of 15 years.

BELOW: *The signing of the Treaty of Versailles was a major world event. Finally, the war was officially over.*

REPARATIONS AND THE WAR GUILT CLAUSE

One of the most **controversial** demands of the treaty was that Germany pay reparations. Reparations were sums of money paid to the Allied countries to make up for the cost of the war. Under the Treaty of Versailles, Germany was expected to pay what today would equal five billion American dollars.

But perhaps the most famous and most important section of the treaty was Article 231, also known as the **War Guilt Clause**. This clause said that Germany had to take full responsibility for the war, including the cost, destruction, and casualties. The War Guilt Clause had a major impact on Germans. It was viewed as a national humiliation and created a feeling of resentment toward the Allied countries that carried into WWII.

> " It is a very severe settlement with Germany, but there is not anything in it that she did not earn. "
>
> —WOODROW WILSON, EXPLAINING THE TREATY TO AMERICANS

What do you think?
Did Germany deserve to be punished for the war? What other steps could Germany have taken to repay the Allied countries?

BELOW: *Signing the Treaty of Versailles*

AN UNHAPPY PEACE

Germany's leaders did not want to sign the Treaty of Versailles because they had no say about what went into it. They agreed to sign it only if some of the demands were removed. For example, the Allies wanted to send the former German emperor Kaiser Wilhelm to trial for the crime of starting the war. German leaders found this unacceptable. They also did not want to pay reparations. When the German leaders refused to sign under these terms, the Allies gave them 24 hours to change their minds, or their country would be invaded. Germany signed the treaty.

Views on the Treaty of Versailles were mixed. For the French, it didn't go far enough. The French newspaper *Le Temps* ran an editorial arguing that the treaty was flawed because it failed to "destroy the unity of Germany." The British were more enthusiastic, and David Lloyd George was welcomed home in triumph.

RIGHT: *At the time, most people were aware of Germany's anger at being forced to sign the treaty.*

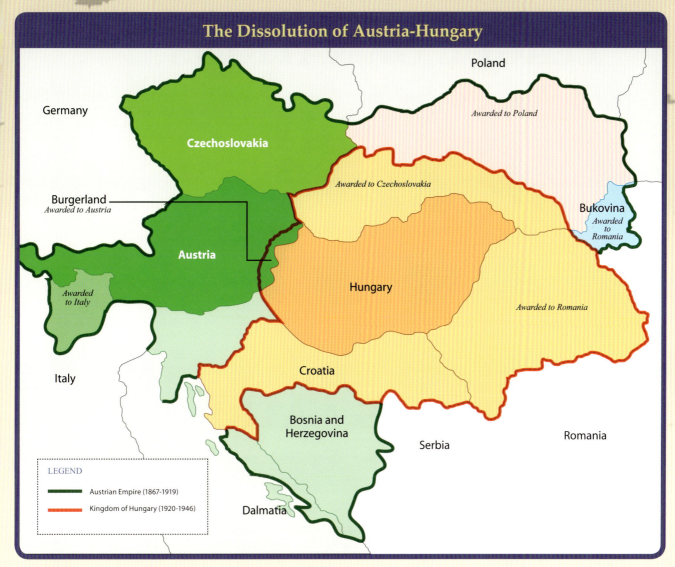

ABOVE: *This map shows how Austria was split up according to the Treaty of Saint-Germain-en-Laye.*

OTHER TREATIES

The Treaty of Versailles was only one of the post-war treaties. The **Treaty of Saint-Germain-en-Laye, Treaty of Trianon,** and **Treaty of Sevres** played an important role in re-drawing the map of Europe.

These treaties called for the end of the Austro-Hungarian and Ottoman empires. This meant that many countries were given independence, including Armenia, Czechoslovakia, Greece, Hungary, Poland, and Yugoslavia. It also meant that the empires of Britain, France, and Italy were expanded, because they were given land in the Middle East.

LEFT: *This was the original League of Nations logo.*

THE LEAGUE OF NATIONS

Woodrow Wilson believed passionately that the League of Nations could settle disagreements between **rival** countries before they could go to war with each other. But many Americans believed they had spent too much money and lost too many soldiers in WWI—a war that didn't even concern them. Some Americans believed that the United States shouldn't get involved in world affairs at all. Because of American isolationism, Congress refused to allow the United States to join the League of Nations.

Much like the United Nations of today, the League needed all the countries in the world to join for the organization to be effective. The loss of the United States was a heavy blow to the League. Even worse was the fact that according to the Treaty of Versailles, Germany was not allowed to join. The War Guilt Clause stated that Germany was no longer a part of the international community. This left Germany feeling like an outsider. Russia was also not allowed to join.

What Do You Know?

The United Nations today is a much better version of the League of Nations. Founded just after World War II, it allows all countries to be involved. Even nations that aren't member states can go to the UN to debate and settle disagreements. Though far from perfect, the United Nations comes much closer to fulfilling Woodrow Wilson's ideal than the original League of Nations did.

GOOD INTENTIONS

The treaties created after WWI were made to prevent another war. They gave independence to some countries, and tried to create an international League of Nations. But because of the harsh terms the Treaty of Versailles put on Germany, and the lack of support for the League, the treaties failed to make a lasting peace. Instead, they humiliated Germany and created a less stable Europe.

Doomed to Failure

Germany, Russia, and the United States were three of the largest and most powerful countries in the world, even after World War I. Without their support, the League of Nations that was formed on January 10, 1920, was doomed to fail. Despite being created to prevent war, the League was powerless to prevent World War II.

RIGHT: *This political cartoon shows how unpopular the League was in America.*

CHAPTER 2

POLITICAL SHIFTS POST-WWI

Europe began to change a lot after World War I. There were new countries, and new **political** ideas started to become popular and spread throughout the continent. In many countries, **charismatic** leaders promising bold changes started to take power. These changes contributed to the economic and political conflicts that were, in part, a cause of World War II.

COMMUNIST RUSSIA

During WWI, Russia's monarchy was overthrown and replaced by a Communist government. Communists believed that the workers, not politicians or kings, should rule a country. They believed that there should be no **private property**, and that everyone should share all the wealth equally. In Russia, the Communist government was called the Soviet government.

There were many people in Russia who did not want communism, however. Groups with different political beliefs protested against the Soviet government, and soon the country was fighting a civil war.

The Soviet leader was a man called Lenin. To lead the civil war against his rivals, Lenin began to take more and more power away from the Russian people.

LENIN
(1870–1924)

Vladimir Ilyich Ulyanov, more commonly known as Lenin, was the leader of the Communist party in Russia. Born to a wealthy family, he became interested in communism while at university and began protesting against the **tsar**. In 1917, he and Leon Trotsky led a revolution which established the first communist state of Russia. Eventually, they joined other communist states and formed the Soviet Union in 1922.

From Communism to Dictatorship

In 1924, Lenin died of a stroke and Joseph Stalin took over. Stalin's communism was more like a dictatorship. He was a harsh ruler who killed or imprisoned anyone who disagreed with him, including his own citizens. Stalin believed in holding absolute power over the Russian people. He controlled all of the newspapers, the military, and the police. He is most remembered for his terrible **purges**, during which he killed hundreds of thousands of people.

Both Germany and the Allies recognized that the Soviet Union was a powerful player, even if they disagreed with communism. As tensions grew between the Axis and the Allies, both sides raced to make an alliance with Stalin. Even Germany, an old enemy, offered to make peace with the new Soviet government.

This made the Americans very nervous. American president Franklin Roosevelt hated Stalin and called Soviet Russia a "dictatorship as absolute as any other dictatorship in the world." But even Roosevelt knew the Allies couldn't defeat Germany without Russia's help. Russia was a huge country, with plenty of natural resources, including iron ore, wood, and coal. Those resources would be very useful in a war. Russia also had a large army, with an estimated 20 million men.

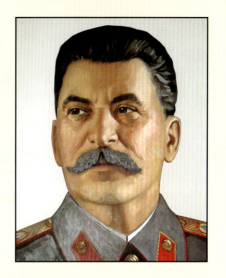

JOSEPH STALIN
(1878–1953)

Iosif Vissarionovich Dzhugashvili, more commonly known as Stalin, was ruler of the Union of Soviet Socialist Republics before and during World War II. Born to illiterate peasants in the country now known as Georgia, Stalin quickly rose through the ranks of the Communist Party. He was known for using underhanded tactics and forming secret alliances. He also created the famous **Gulags**, horrible prison camps where people were sentenced to hard labor. Today, he is remembered as a tyrant responsible for the deaths of millions of people.

JAPAN DURING WWI

During World War I, Japan fought on the side of the Allies because it had signed the **Anglo-Japanese Alliance** with the British in 1902. The agreement stated that if either Britain or Japan went to war, the other country would help them.

However, for a long time, Japan had wanted to conquer parts of China and gain control of its rich resources. In 1915, when China was weak, the powerful Japanese sent the Chinese government a list of 21 Demands. It included a demand that China give over parts of Manchuria, which was in the north, to Japanese control. The Chinese had no way to fight against a Japanese invasion, so they gave in.

After the war, Japan's confidence grew. At the time, Japan was a dictatorship, ruled by the powerful Emperor Showa, and it had a strong military. Many high-ranking Japanese were the descendants of wealthy samurai households.

> **What do you think?**
> Look at the difference between the Japanese flag during the time of imperialism and the Japanese flag today. What do you think the differences mean?

ABOVE: *The flag of the Imperial Japanese Navy and the Japan Maritime Self-Defense Force, 1889–1945*

RIGHT: *This was proclaimed as the national Japanese flag in 1999.*

RIGHT: *Emperor Showa, better known as Hirohito, reigned in Japan from 1926 until his death in 1989.*

Imperialist Japan

By the time Japan went to the Paris Peace Conference, it was ready to demand a more active role in world affairs. Japan wanted two main things from the peace conference. The first was control of some of the colonies that Germany had lost during the war. The second was to include a **Racial Equality Provision** in the **charter** of the League of Nations. The Japanese were tired of the Europeans treating them as inferior. This new provision would ensure that they were treated the same as everyone else. The Japanese were disappointed when The Big Three refused both demands.

The Japanese felt left out by the West, and they began to think that the only way to earn respect was through military takeover. This led to the rise of **imperialism** in Japan. Imperialism occurs when one country forcefully takes over or rules another country's territory, or sometimes the entire country. For Japan, this meant taking over China, as well as other territories. But to achieve that goal, Japan's military had to be strong. Japanese society soon became **militaristic**, with most of the power and wealth being transferred to the army.

Just like Stalin, the emperor and his generals began to crack down on those who disagreed with them. In 1925, they enacted the **Peace Preservation Law**, which made it illegal to be a communist or democrat. Soon the combination of these forces would turn Japan from an important ally into a bitter enemy of the West.

ITALY DURING WWI

Like the Japanese, the Italians were allies of Britain and France during World War I. But for them, the war was much more difficult. One out of every three Italian soldiers were killed during the war, versus one out of every ten American soldiers. So when the Paris Peace Conference began, the Italians wanted to be rewarded for their sacrifice.

Like Japan, the Italians were disappointed by the outcome of the conference. They felt they did not get fair treatment. Territory they felt belonged to them was given to other countries. In particular, the town of Fiume, which had mostly Italian-speaking citizens, was given to the Kingdom of Yugoslavia.

At home, the Italians were very unhappy with their government. Between 1919 and 1922, there were five different prime ministers. The economy was failing. As riots began to erupt, one man promised to unify the Italian people. He was Benito Mussolini, and he founded the National Fascist Party.

> **Did You Know?**
> By the time of World War I, Italy had only been a country for 43 years. Before that, each Italian city was considered its own country.

BELOW: *Mussolini and the key leaders of the March on Rome*

Italian Fascism

Mussolini was a charismatic leader. He inspired two new feelings among the Italian people. The first was **nationalism**, the belief that one's country is the best country in the world. The second was **militarism**. Like the Japanese, Mussolini believed Italy should have a strong military force. **Fascism** is the combination of extreme nationalism and extreme militarism. Usually, fascist governments are controlled by a dictator.

Mussolini took advantage of the Italian people's dislike of their government. He convinced them that if he were in power, he would improve the economy and further Italy's interests. Mussolini led an army of fascist rebels in the March on Rome on October 29, 1922. The next day, the king of Italy removed his crown and made Mussolini the new ruler.

BENITO MUSSOLINI
(1883–1945)

Benito Amilcare Andrea Mussolini was born the son of a blacksmith in a small Italian village. When he was a young man, he ran away to Switzerland to avoid having to serve in the army. When he came back, he began a political career as a fascist. He brought Italians together and established a dictatorship.

GERMANY AFTER WWI

After World War I, Germany was in a bad state. The punishments imposed by the Treaty of Versailles were taking a toll. The high reparations meant that the government had very little money to rebuild what was destroyed in Germany during the war. Many Germans didn't have jobs. There was also a severe food shortage in the country, leading to widespread starvation. All of this made the German people very dissatisfied with the government.

In addition, a rumor spread that the government had betrayed the German people during the war and had lost the war on purpose. This became known as the "stab-in-the-back" myth. Many angry Germans believed that the government did not provide the German army with the food, weapons, and money it needed to defeat the Allies. They felt a change in government was needed. It was the perfect time for Adolf Hitler to take control.

ADOLF HITLER
(1889–1945)

Adolf Hitler was the founder of the Nazi Party and the leader of Germany during World War II. He was an intense and charismatic leader, known for delivering inspiring speeches. He was also a violent and evil man. He hated everyone who was not a German, and all Jewish people, even if they were German citizens. Together with his generals, he killed more than six million Jews before the war was over. Hitler committed suicide on April 30, 1945, a few days before the Allies took over Berlin.

Germany Under Hitler

Adolf Hitler's deep nationalism became very popular with German people at the time. Hitler gave Germans a common enemy. This made them feel more united than they felt under the old government. Hitler attacked the Jewish people and other minorities such as Jehovah's Witnesses, homosexuals, communists, and people with disabilities.

What Do You Know?

In Canada during World War I, an enraged population went as far as to put thousands of its own citizens into forced labor camps, simply because they were of German or Austrian-Hungarian descent. As World War I continued, anti-German feelings only became worse. In Britain, hatred of Germans became so strong that the Royal Family had to change its name from the German name Saxe-Coburg to Windsor.

As the Nazi political party became more popular, German president Paul von Hindenburg decided to use Hitler to control the German people. He offered to make Hitler the vice-chancellor of Germany. Hitler boldly demanded to be made chancellor. Hindenburg believed that Hitler was a great speaker, but not a smart man. He thought he could control Hitler. He made Hitler the chancellor in January 1933. Hindenburg died the next year, and Hitler took control of Germany.

Just like the leaders of Japan, Italy, and the Soviet Union at the time, Hitler began to imprison or execute anyone who stood in his way. He was ready to start another war, to win back what he believed the Allies had taken from Germany.

RIGHT: *Hitler was a great speaker and was able to convince Germans that he would be a good leader.*

CHAPTER 3

THE GREAT DEPRESSION AND GLOBAL ECONOMIC DECLINE

THE GREAT DEPRESSION

Often, when a country's economy is failing, citizens believe that a change in government will help. In times of hardship when people don't have adequate jobs or enough food on the table, they turn to radical leaders who are able to take advantage of the people's anger. In 1929, a worldwide economic slump began that is known as the **Great Depression**.

> *What do you think?*
> Why would a country in economic hardship want a fascist or communist government?

THE ROARING TWENTIES AND BLACK TUESDAY

From 1920 to 1929, many of the former Allied countries experienced a boost in their economy. Industry was strong, people had lots of money, and things looked promising. Part of this prosperity was due to the stock market. The stock market allows people from across the world to buy and sell pieces of companies, known as shares. When a company is doing well, the value of its shares goes up. During the 1920s, the shares of most companies were very high in value. This period of time is known as the **Roaring Twenties**.

A stock market can also crash. This happens when the values of shares fall suddenly and unexpectedly. On Tuesday October 29, 1929, the biggest crash in the history of the stock market happened. This famous crash is known as Black Tuesday.

LEFT: *This is a photograph of Wall Street shortly after Black Tuesday.*

THE EFFECTS OF THE GREAT DEPRESSION

When the stock market crashed on Black Tuesday, millions of people went bankrupt. Many people had bought shares in the hopes that the Roaring Twenties would continue into the 1930s, and that they could later sell the shares for more than they had paid. But now the shares were worthless, and the money was gone.

Because the stock market was used internationally, nearly every country on the globe was affected by the crash. That led to a ten-year period known as the Great Depression. The 1930s were mostly shaped by how different governments responded to the crisis.

The United States

More than 12 million people in the United States were left without jobs at the height of the Great Depression. This led to widespread hunger, with many people spending whole days waiting in lines just to buy bread. It also changed American politics. In 1933, President Franklin D. Roosevelt was elected, and he began a program called the **New Deal**.

The extreme poverty in the United States was part of the reason America waited for two years to join Britain and France after they declared war on Germany in 1939. Most Americans believed the United States didn't have the money to spend on weapons and equipment.

RIGHT: *One of the programs President Roosevelt started was the Work Progress Administration (WPA). The WPA employed millions of people to build public buildings and roads.*

Britain

Britain was still rebuilding from WWI when the Depression hit. Soon after, people overseas could not afford to buy British goods. Nearly one in five British people became jobless. The British were able to recover from the Depression more easily than the Americans, however. The main reason for Britain's quicker recovery was because it abandoned the Gold Standard. A country using the Gold Standard determines how much its money is worth based on how much gold it has. By abandoning this method, Britain was able to make its money worth less. That made it cheaper to buy British goods, and helped the economy.

Canada

The Depression hit Canada even harder than it hit elsewhere. In addition to the stock market crash, Canada also experienced a long drought that destroyed its farming industry. With no food to grow, there was no food to sell, and the economy sank. One in three Canadians were unemployed. In the Canadian prairies, people's income dropped by as much as 90 percent.

ABOVE: *The 1930s became known as the Dirty Thirties, partly because the drought left nothing but dust in the prairies.*

Russia

Because Russia had a Communist government, there was no stock market. Russia, too, had economic problems, but it was not really affected by the Great Depression. Because everyone worked for the state, there was no real unemployment. Instead, people worked long, hard hours for very little pay and food. No other country would trade with the communist government. This caused great economic strain on the population.

Japan

The Depression did not greatly affect Japan. The Japanese were able to quickly **devalue** their currency, which made their goods cheaper. Soon, they were even selling silk to the British. Sound financial planning saved the Japanese economy.

Germany

The German economy was in bad shape after WWI, and the Depression only made it worse. The reparations established by the Treaty of Versailles were impossible to pay. In 1924, the Allies enacted the Dawes Plan, which demanded that Germany pay more than one billion marks each year. Then they enacted the Young Plan in 1929. The plan reduced the amount, but it was still impossible for Germany to pay. To survive the 1920s, Germany had to borrow money from the Americans. When the stock market crashed in 1929, America called in the debt. Germany could not pay.

BELOW: *Even children worked in Soviet Russia. Here, children dig up frozen potatoes on a collective farm in 1933.*

INVASIONS AND OCCUPATIONS

CHAPTER 4

Throughout the 1920s and 1930s, Germany, Italy, and Japan invaded several other countries to increase their wealth, natural resources, and power. They had been growing their armies and preparing themselves for a coming war. Although other nations, such as Britain and the United States, were worried about these invasions, they did little to stop them. They were busy rebuilding after WWI, and didn't have the resources for more fighting.

ITALY INVADES CORFU

By 1923, Mussolini had won over the Italian people by promising them a return to Italy's glorious past, represented by the Roman Empire. He wanted to expand Italy's borders, but that required the use of force.

After an Italian general was assassinated by unknown Greeks, Mussolini sent his navy to bombard the tiny Greek island of Corfu. Sixteen civilians were killed before the League of Nations **intervened**. Greece was forced to pay 50 million Italian lire and formally apologize to Italy. In exchange, the Italians left Corfu.

ITALY INVADES ETHIOPIA

Mussolini's next step was to invade the African country of Ethiopia, also known then as Abyssinia. In the late 1800s, Italy had lost a war in Ethiopia. Mussolini wanted to win Ethiopia back to restore Italy's reputation. In 1934, a **skirmish** between Ethiopian and Italian forces took place on the border of Ethiopia. Two hundred Italian soldiers were killed. In 1935, Mussolini used this as an excuse to attack. The League of Nations **condemned** the attack, but did nothing to stop it. Mussolini conquered Ethiopia in just seven months.

ITALY INVADES ALBANIA

Italy invaded Albania in 1939, just before WWII began. The two countries were allies before the invasion. Albania allowed Italy to use its resources, and Italy loaned money to Albania. But

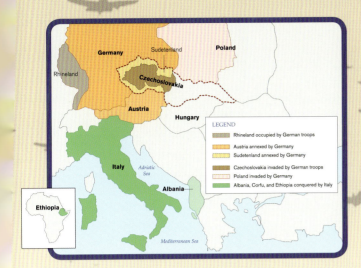

ABOVE: *This map shows the territory Germany and Italy claimed before WWII began.*

GERMANY OCCUPIES THE RHINELAND

To most Germans, the Treaty of Versailles was an insult. One of its articles stated that Germany was not allowed to have any military presence in a strip of land called Rhineland.

Rhineland bordered on many countries, including France and Belgium. This made it an easy place for Germany to launch an invasion against France, and which made the French nervous about allowing Germany to control it. German civilians were allowed to live and work in Rhineland, but French, British, and American forces controlled it.

In 1936, Adolf Hitler began to fulfill his promise of getting revenge for the German people. He violated the Treaty of Versailles and illegally rebuilt the German army. He moved his army into Rhineland. This was the first sign that he was preparing for war. And with the Depression at its height, the British government was too busy handling crises at home to deal with foreign wars. Britain had always thought the treaty was too harsh on Germany anyway, so it let the Germans occupy Rhineland to avoid another war.

over Albania because it would give him control over who entered the Adriatic Sea. So, when Hitler invaded Czechoslovakia without telling Mussolini, Mussolini invaded Albania. He thought this would prove to Hitler that Italy was a strong ally.

THE LEAGUE RESPONDS

After these invasions, the League of Nations responded, but not very strongly. It stated that Italy could not receive important goods from other countries, and that other countries could not buy goods from Italy. The goal was to hurt Italy's economy. By that time, however, it was too late. Italy had already taken over the lands it needed.

LEFT: *Kurt von Schuschnigg, the chancellor of Austria who surrendered to Hitler*

GERMANY OCCUPIES AUSTRIA AND SUDETENLAND

During WWI, Germany and Austria were allies and became very powerful. Then the Treaty of Versailles banned Germany from having an alliance with Austria. In 1938, Hitler found a way around that rule: he invaded Austria.

First, he invited the Austrian chancellor Kurt von Schuschnigg for talks. Schuschnigg wanted no part of an alliance with Hitler, but Hitler threatened to invade. He forced Schuschnigg to put high-ranking Nazis in the Austrian government. With Hitler in control of Rhineland, the Austrians were afraid. On March 11, Schuschnigg surrendered and Austria became a part of Germany.

Hitler's next step was to take over Sudetenland, which was controlled by Czechoslovakia at the time. Sudetenland already had a large German population, and Hitler believed the region rightfully belonged to Germany. In 1938, he began encouraging Nazis in Sudetenland to rebel against the Czechoslovakian government.

The Czechoslovakian government was furious and cracked down on Nazi supporters in the region. British prime minister Neville Chamberlain was afraid war would break out. He arranged to meet with Hitler. On behalf of the League of Nations, he gave Germany Sudetenland in exchange for a promise that Hitler would not go to war. This was called the **Munich Agreement**.

GERMANY INVADES POLAND

Hitler had no intention of keeping the promise he made in the Munich Agreement. In 1939, he invaded Poland. He had no fear of the Soviet Union coming to help Poland, because the Nazis and the Soviets had agreed not to fight one another. With more than 2,000 tanks, 1,000 planes, and countless soldiers, the Nazi army crushed the Polish defenses in weeks. Britain and France declared war on Germany on September 3, 1939.

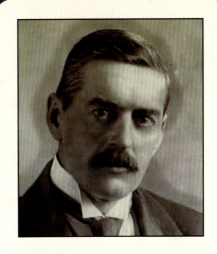

NEVILLE CHAMBERLAIN
(1869–1940)

Arthur Neville Chamberlain was the British prime minister from 1937 to 1940. He was born into a family of politicians. His father and brother were both Members of Parliament. Today, he is best remembered for his policy of **appeasement**. This means that he was willing to give in to Hitler's breaking of the Treaty of Versailles, if it would avoid war. Historians still debate whether the policy was better or worse in the long run than trying to punish Hitler.

> " You can imagine what a bitter blow it is to me that all my long struggle to win peace has failed. Yet I cannot believe that there is anything more or anything different that I could have done and that would have been more successful. "
> —NEVILLE CHAMBERLAIN, COMMENTING ON HIS NEGOTIATIONS WITH HITLER

RIGHT: *This map shows the new territory Japan controlled after it took over Manchuria.*

JAPAN INVADES MANCHURIA

In 1931, Japan had an exploding population. The country needed more land, resources, and wealth. Japan had been interested in taking over parts of China for a long time. In particular, they wanted the region known as Manchuria. Manchuria was more than 77,000 square miles (199,430 square km) and was rich in lumber, minerals, and other natural resources.

The military leaders of Japan did not like people who were not Japanese. In particular, these generals hated the Chinese people. The Japanese army was strong and powerful, and when an explosion occurred on a Japanese-controlled railway in Manchuria, the army blamed the Chinese and invaded Manchuria.

The League of Nations stepped in and demanded that the Japanese withdraw. The Japanese government agreed. However, the army would not listen to the government. This was because of a strong culture of militarism in Japanese society at the time. Japan continued to invade until it had control over all of Manchuria.

This put the League in a difficult position. Its warnings had been ignored. The League could have put **sanctions** on Japan and blocked its trade with other countries, the same way it did with Germany in WWI. But the member countries of the League needed Japan as a trade partner.

THE WEAKNESS OF THE LEAGUE OF NATIONS

The League of Nations compromised. They agreed that the Japanese should leave Manchuria, but that Manchuria should become its own country, instead of being returned to the Chinese. Japan, seeing that the League of Nations was powerless to stop them, dropped out of the League and continued to occupy Manchuria. This was a devastating blow to the reputation of the League. It exposed weaknesses that Hitler and Mussolini later took advantage of.

What do you think?
Was it wise for the League to compromise with Japan? Why or why not?

OUTBREAK OF WAR IN ASIA

In 1937, the Japanese declared a full-scale war with China. The Chinese stood little chance against the Japanese forces because China's army was poorly trained and poorly equipped. The Japanese army took full advantage of that and killed hundreds of thousands of Chinese.

In 1941, Japan angered France by invading its colony of Indochina, which included present-day Cambodia, Laos, parts of Thailand, and Vietnam. The French were busy fighting Germany in Europe and had left their colonies in the Pacific poorly protected. In just three days, the Japanese had taken Vietnam.

RIGHT: *Japanese soldiers in occupied Manchuria*

JAPAN PUTS AN EMBARGO ON CHINA

For the first few years of the war, the United States did not participate. Still recovering from the Great Depression, the country believed it had learned its lesson from World War I. Americans believed the conflict between Britain, France, Germany, and Italy was a European problem.

Soon though, the Americans grew wary of growing threats. After Japan took over Manchuria, the Japanese government put an embargo on all products coming into China. An embargo is similar to a blockade, it prevents goods from coming into a country. Many of these products were American-made military supplies. The United States needed to sell the products, which meant that the embargo was bad for American business.

ABOVE: *Pearl Harbor was a quiet naval base before it was attacked in 1941.*

LEFT: *This photo depicts the destroyer USS* Arizona *exploding during the attack on Pearl Harbor.*

THE UNITED STATES PUTS AN EMBARGO ON JAPAN

In response to the embargo placed on products coming into China, the United States put an embargo on Japan. This prevented the Japanese from buying oil, which it needed to power vehicles and produce electricity. Because Japan could no longer buy oil, it decided to conquer new oil-rich lands in the South China Sea. But there was a problem. Pearl Harbor, an American military base, was close to Japan's targets. The Japanese feared that if they attempted to attack an oil-rich country such as Malaysia, the American fleet would be dispatched to combat them. So instead, the Japanese decided to attack first.

JAPAN ATTACKS PEARL HARBOR

On December 7, 1941, Japanese airplanes began bombing Pearl Harbor. More than 3,500 Americans were killed or wounded, 350 planes were destroyed, and 18 ships were sunk. It was a serious blow to the U.S. Navy. The Japanese believed the attack would scare the Americans and prevent them from becoming involved in the war.

Instead, it had the opposite effect. The Japanese had awoken the "sleeping giant," and on December 8, 1941, the United States joined World War II.

CHAPTER 5
PACTS AND ALLIANCES

Between the two World Wars, countries made many new alliances and agreements. Some agreements were meant to keep peace. If a small country was allied with a more powerful country, an attack by a third country was less likely, for example. Other pacts, however, were made so that the countries involved could prepare for war, which seemed more and more inevitable.

Agreements were sometimes made to allow countries to build up their armies or store up more weapons. For example, Britain and Germany signed the Anglo-German Naval Agreement in 1935. The agreement allowed Germany to ignore the rule in the Treaty of Versailles against building warships, if Germany kept the numbers of ships in their navy lower than the number of ships in the British navy.

AXIS PACTS

Anti-Comintern Pact
The first important pre-war pact was made between Germany and Japan on November 25, 1936. The Anti-Comintern Pact, as it was called, was an agreement between the fascist Nazis and imperialist Japanese to fight together against communism. Specifically, this meant fighting against the Soviet Union. One year later, Mussolini joined the pact as well, which formed the core of the Axis alliance: Germany, Italy, and Japan.

Pact of Steel
In 1939, two more pacts were made. The first was the **Pact of Steel**, between Italy and Germany. This was an alliance that pledged full mutual support for both countries. In practice, it allowed Hitler to tell Mussolini what to do. Hitler did not want Italy to start a war before he was ready.

Molotov–Ribbentrop Pact
The second pact, signed two months later, was the Nazi–Soviet Pact, also known as the **Molotov–Ribbentrop Pact**. It was an agreement between Nazi Germany and the Soviet Union to equally divide and annex the country of Poland. It was a non-aggression pact, which meant that Germany and the Soviet Union agreed not to fight each other.

Since Hitler no longer had to worry about the Soviet army in eastern Europe, he could focus on preparing for war against countries such as Britain and France in western Europe. With the Nazi–Soviet Pact in place, Hitler didn't have to be concerned about an attack from Russia. That made it easier for Germany to invade Poland in 1939 and to begin World War II.

Tripartite Pact
The Japanese and the Italians were not happy with the Molotov–Ribbentrop Pact, since it broke the rules of the Anti-Comintern Pact. The problem was solved when Germany, Italy, and Japan signed the new **Tripartite Pact** in 1940, in which they agreed to support each other against any enemy.

LEFT: *This photo shows a newly-built German warship being launched. It is ready to join the German navy.*

What do you think?
What made these three countries want to ally with each other?

CONCLUSION

THE LONG ROAD TO WAR

THE TREATY OF VERSAILLES

It is impossible to point to any one event or person as the cause of World War II. Only a combination of events can explain the outbreak of such global violence.

The period between World War I and World War II was a time of major change in the world. When the Big Three met at the Palace of Versailles, they each had their own plans for the future. They argued, made compromises, and tried to settle old disagreements. They met with

ABOVE: *The leaders of the Big Three Allied countries at the Yalta Conference: Winston Churchill (Britain), Franklin Roosevelt (United States), and Joseph Stalin (Soviet Union)*

representatives from countries all over the world to try to make lasting peace. But too often, self-interest got in the way. Important countries such as Russia weren't invited because the Big Three didn't approve of communism. Many small countries that had been colonized by big European nations didn't have a voice at all. The Treaty of Versailles left few people happy. Germany was humiliated and punished through the War Guilt Clause and the weight of reparations. The Italians were denied lands they believed rightfully belonged to them.

The creation of the League of Nations was a first step toward building an international community. But the League was flawed from the beginning. Germany was not allowed to join. That prevented Germany from participating in international discussions and left many of its citizens feeling isolated from the rest of the world. Many Germans felt they were treated like second-class citizens by the Big Three. Saddled with debt and full of anger, the Germans turned to Adolf Hitler and the fascist Nazi party. Hitler rose to power through fear, secrecy, and by taking advantage of the German people's suffering.

RADICAL CHANGES AND THE GREAT DEPRESSION

Italy, too, turned to fascism. Mussolini's March on Rome was a success, and soon there was talk of Italy becoming a world power. Elsewhere, a bloody civil war in the Soviet Union gave rise to the vicious Joseph Stalin. Meanwhile, Japan's imperialist army generals were plotting to dominate Asia.

These threats were made even worse by the Great Depression. Germany was broke, America was crippled, Canada was hungry, riots erupted in Paris. In the midst of economic desperation, Hitler and the other Axis leaders began to start small wars. The League of Nations didn't have the money or resources to stop them. Soon the League was revealed to be powerless, and Hitler and his allies became bolder.

What do you think?
What could have been done differently to prevent the war? How would you have changed the treaties?

EVENTS LEADING TO WORLD WAR II

Date	Event	Summary
March 16, 1917	Russian Revolution	The tsar is overthrown, and Russia becomes communist.
January 18, 1918	Paris Peace Conference	The Peace Conference begins, and the Big Three begin drafting the Treaty of Versailles.
November 11, 1918	Armistice Day	Germany signs the Armistice of Compiègne and surrenders to the Triple Entente.
June 28, 1919	Treaty of Versailles signed	Germany signs the Treaty of Versailles, and WWI officially ends.
October 29, 1922	March on Rome	Mussolini leads an army to the capital and overthrows the king of Italy.
August 29, 1923	Corfu Incident	Italy invades the Greek island of Corfu.
September 18, 1931	Invasion of Manchuria	Japan attacks the Chinese region of Manchuria.
August 19, 1934	Hitler begins his rise to power.	Adolf Hitler, already chancellor, is also elected president of Germany. That gives him absolute power.
October 3, 1935	Second Italo-Ethiopian War	Italy invades Ethiopia.
March 7, 1936	Invasion of Rhineland	Hitler occupies Rhineland with German troops.
November 25, 1936	Anti-Comintern Pact is signed.	Germany signs a treaty with Japan.
July 7, 1937	Second Sino-Japanese War	Japan declares war on China.
March 12, 1938	Annexation of Austria	Germany takes over Austria.
May 22, 1939	Pact of Steel signed	Germany allies with Italy.
September 1, 1939	Invasion of Poland	German forces invade Poland.
September 2, 1939	The Allies declare war on Germany.	France and Britain go to war against Germany.
September 22, 1940	Japan declares war on Indochina.	Japanese forces invade French-controlled Indochina, beginning the war in Asia.
September 27, 1940	Tripartite Act signed	Japan, Italy, and Germany agree to fight for each other.
December 7, 1941	Japan attacks the United States	The Japanese bomb the American naval base at Pearl Harbor.
December 8, 1941	United States declares war on Japan	The United States declares war against the Axis powers.

FURTHER READING AND WEBSITES

BOOKS

Adams, Simon. *World War II.* DK Children, 2007.

Wagner, Margaret E., et al. (eds.). *World War II Companion.* Simon & Shuster, 2007.

Panchyk, Richard. *World War II for Kids: A History with 21 Activities.* Chicago Review Press, 2002.

Jeffrey, Gary. *Battle for the Atlantic.* Crabtree Publishing Company, 2012.

Jeffrey, Gary. *North Africa and the Mediterranean.* Crabtree Publishing Company, 2012.

Jeffrey, Gary. *The Eastern Front.* Crabtree Publishing Company, 2012.

Jeffrey, Gary. *The Secret War.* Crabtree Publishing Company, 2012.

Jeffrey, Gary. *The Western Front.* Crabtree Publishing Company, 2012.

Jeffrey, Gary. *War in the Pacific.* Crabtree Publishing Company, 2012.

WEBSITES

World War Two - Causes
www.historyonthenet.com/ww2/causes.htm
This website provides an easy-to-understand, step-by-step breakdown of the events leading to WWII.

Signing the Treaty of Versailles, 1919
eyewitnesstohistory.com/versailles.htm
This website includes a report on the signing of the Treaty of Versailles — from someone who was actually there!

AUTHOR BIOGRAPHY

Alexander Offord is a playwright and author from Toronto, Canada. He has written two books for children, and his plays have been staged all across Canada and the United States. He currently lives in Toronto.

GLOSSARY

Allied powers a group of countries that fought together during World War I (led by British Empire, French Republic, and Russian Empire), and World War II (led by Britain, France, the Soviet Union, and the United States)

Anglo-Japanese Alliance an alliance between Britain and Japan which stated that if either country went to war, the other country would help

annexation an act by which one country forcefully takes control over another country's territory

appeasement the act of agreeing to something you would not normally agree to for the purpose of keeping peace

atomic bomb a powerful explosive device first developed and used at the end of World War II

Armistice of Compiègne the formal agreement that ended World War I, signed at 11 a.m. on November 11, 1918

Axis powers a group of countries that fought together during World War I (led by the German Empire, Austria-Hungary, and the Ottoman Empire), and World War II (led by Germany, Italy, and Japan)

charismatic charming, attractive, having a strong character

charter a written list of rights, privileges, and responsibilities

civilians people who are not in the armed forces

colony a country controlled by a stronger country that uses the colony's resources for its own benefit

condemned said in a strong way that someone or something was wrong

controversial causing disagreement or argument

devalue a downward adjustment to the value of a country's currency

Fascism the combination of extreme nationalism and extreme militarism

fronts the line between two enemies fighting a war

Great Depression a period in the 1930s in which many countries had failing economies, which led to millions of people losing their jobs and going hungry

Gulags horrible prison camps in Russia where people were sentenced to hard labor

Holocaust the mass murder of people, often referring to the Jewish Holocaust, the period in WWII when the Nazis murdered six million Jewish people

imperialism a policy of expanding a nation's power and influence over other countries

Inquiry a group of 150 experts who were asked to figure out the best way to ensure peace after WWI. They wrote the Fourteen Points.

intervened got involved to prevent or alter a course of events

isolationism a policy of not participating in the affairs of other countries

League of Nations an international organization formed after WWI, similar to today's United Nations

mandate an official order to do something

militarism when the army has the highest degree of respect and support in the country, even more than the government

militaristic having an aggressive military policy

Molotov–Ribbentrop Pact the agreement signed between Germany and the Soviet Union before WWII in which the two nations agreed to share Poland. Also known as the Nazi–Soviet Pact.

Munich Agreement an agreement between British prime minister Neville Chamberlain and Hitler, which gave Germany Sudetenland in exchange for a promise from Hitler that he would not go to war

nationalism extreme pride in your own nation, especially a feeling that your country is superior to all others

New Deal a series of economic policies and programs designed to help the American economy recover from the Great Depression

Ottoman Empire a large and powerful Turkish empire that was broken up following its defeat in WWI

Pact of Steel an agreement made between Italy and Germany in 1939, in which the two countries pledged full support to one another

Paris Peace Conference an international conference held following the end of WWI to discuss the future of the world; where the Treaty of Versailles was created

Peace Preservation Law a law enacted in Japan in 1925 which made it illegal to be a democrat or communist; a law to punish people who didn't agree with the emperor and his generals

political relating to the government or public affairs of a country

private property land that is owned by an individual as opposed to land owned by the public

purges a series of violent removals of a group of people from a place, often involving mass murder

Racial Equality Provision a part of the League of Nations charter proposed by the Japanese government that said all member states deserve equal and just treatment, regardless of race or nationality

rival someone who tries to defeat or be more successful than another

Roaring Twenties a period of economic growth experienced by many nations during the 1920s

sanctions penalties for doing something that is against the rules, often in terms of international politics

skirmish a brief or minor fight during a war

treaties formal agreements between countries

Treaty of Saint-Germain-en-Laye the peace agreement between the Allies and the Republic of German-Austria. It was signed on September 10, 1919.

Treaty of Sevres the peace agreement between the Allies and the Ottoman Empire. It was signed on August 10, 1920.

Treaty of Trianon the peace agreement between the Allies and the Kingdom of Hungary. It was signed on June 4, 1920.

Treaty of Versailles the agreement signed at the end of the Paris Peace Conference, which formally ended WWI

Tripartite Pact an agreement between Germany, Italy, and Japan to support each other, signed in 1940

tsar the emperor of Russia before the Russian Revolution

United Nations the international organization founded shortly after WWII and which followed the League of Nations

War Guilt Clause a part of the Treaty of Versailles that stated Germany had to take full responsibility for WWI, including the cost, destruction, and casualties

INDEX

Albania 32–33
alliances 8, 21, 34, 40–41
Allied powers (Allies) 4, 6, 8, 10, 11, 14, 15, 16, 21, 22, 24, 26, 27, 28, 40, 42
    see also Britain, France, United States, Russia
Anti-Comintern Pact 41
Austria 6, 7, 17, 34
Austria-Hungary 4, 5, 17
Axis powers 4, 6, 8, 11, 12, 21, 41
    see also Germany, Italy, Japan

Big Three 12, 23, 42, 43
Britain
    in Allied powers 4, 8
    declaration of war on Germany 8, 29, 35
    during the Great Depression 30
    end of WWI 5, 10
    League of Nations 13
    rationing in 5, 11

Canada 4, 7, 8, 27, 30, 43
Chamberlain, Neville 35
China 14, 22–23, 36, 37–39
Clemenceau, Georges 12
colonies 7, 10, 13, 14, 23, 37
Communism and communists 20–21, 23, 27, 28, 31, 41, 43
Corfu 32, 33
Czechoslovakia 14, 17, 33, 34

embargos 38–39
Emperor Showa (Hirohito) 22, 23
Ethiopia 32, 33

fascism and fascists 24, 25, 41, 43
Ferdinand, Archduke Franz 6
France
    in Allied powers 4, 8
    declaration of war on Germany 8, 29, 35
    end of WWI 10
    German coal mines and 14
    Indochina 37

Germany
    Adolf Hitler 26–27, 33, 34, 35, 37, 41, 43
    annexation of Austria 7, 34
    in Axis powers 4, 8, 41
    coal mines to France 14
    colonies 14
    declaration of war on 29, 35
    Great Depression 31
    invasion of Poland 8, 35, 41
    invasion of Rhineland 33
    League of Nations 18, 43
    naval blockade against 11
    occupation of Sudetenland 34
    reparations 11, 15, 16, 26, 31, 43
    resentment toward Allies 11, 15, 26
    Soviet Union 21, 35, 41
    after WWI 10–11, 26–27
Great Depression 6, 28–31, 33, 38, 43
Greece 7, 17, 32

Hindenburg, Paul von 27
Hirohito (Showa), Emperor 22, 23
Hitler, Adolf 26–27, 33, 34, 35, 37, 41, 43
Holocaust 9, 26, 27
Hungary 4, 5, 7, 17, 33

imperialism and imperialists 22, 23, 41, 43
isolationism 11, 18
Italy
    in Allied powers 4
    in Axis powers 8, 41
    invasions 32–33
    Pact of Steel 41
    during WWI 4, 24–25

Japan
    in Allied powers 4, 22–23
    attack on Pearl Harbor 39
    in Axis powers 8, 41
    invading China 22, 36, 37–38
    Emperor Showa 22, 23
    imperialism 22, 23, 41, 43
    invading Indochina 37
    invading Manchuria 22, 36, 38
    militarism in 22, 23, 25, 36, 43
    Paris Peace Conference 23
    during WWI 4, 22–23
Jewish people 9, 26, 27

League of Nations 7, 13, 18–19, 23, 32, 33, 35, 36–37, 43
Lenin 20–21
Lloyd George, David 10, 12, 16

Manchuria 22, 36–37, 38
March on Rome 23, 24, 43
Molotov–Ribbentrop Pact 41
Mussolini, Benito 24–25, 32, 33, 37, 41, 43

Nazi political party 27, 34, 41, 43

New Deal 29

Ottoman Empire 4, 17

Pacific region 9, 37
Pact of Steel 41
pacts 40–41
Paris Peace Conference 12–13, 14, 23, 24
Pearl Harbor 38, 39
Poland 7, 8, 17, 33, 35, 41

rationing 5, 11
reparations 15, 16, 26, 31, 43
Rhineland 33, 34
Roosevelt, Franklin 21, 29, 42
Russia 4, 8, 18, 20–21, 31

Schuschnigg, Kurt von 34
Soviet Union 7, 20, 21, 27, 35, 41, 42, 43
Stalin, Joseph 21, 23, 43
Sudetenland 33, 34–35

treaties 10–19
Tripartite Pact 41
Treaty of Versailles 14–16, 18, 19, 31, 33, 34, 40, 42–43

United States
    in Allied powers 4, 8
    and Great Depression 29
    isolationism in 11, 18
    Japanese attack on 39
    League of Nations 18
    Soviet Russia 21
    in WWI 11, 18
    in WWII 29, 39

War Guilt Clause 15, 18, 43
Wilhelm, Kaiser 16
Wilson, Woodrow 12, 13, 18
World War I (WWI)
    attitudes after 10–11
    end of 4, 5, 6, 10, 12
    legacy of 5–7
    spending on 11
World War II (WWII)
    beginning of 8–9, 41
    causes of 14, 42–44
    declaration of war on Germany 35
    scale of destruction 9

Yugoslavia 17, 24